Occupational Safety and Health Act of 1970

"To assure safe and healthful working conditions for working men and women; by authorizing enforcement of the standards developed under the Act; by assisting and encouraging the States in their efforts to assure safe and healthful working conditions; by providing for research, information, education, and training in the field of occupational safety and health..."

This informational booklet is intended to provide an overview of frequently cited OSHA standards in the construction industry. This publication does not alter or determine compliance responsibilities, which are set forth in OSHA standards and the *Occupational Safety and Health Act*.

Employers and workers in the 27 states and territories that operate their own OSHA-approved workplace safety and health plans should check with their state safety and health agency. Their state may be enforcing standards and other procedures that, while "at least as effective as" Federal OSHA standards, are not always identical to the federal requirements. For more information on states with OSHA-approved state plans, please visit: www.osha.gov/dcsp/osp.

This information will be made available to sensory-impaired individuals upon request. Voice phone: (202) 693-1999; teletypewriter (TTY) number: 1-877-889-5627.

Cover photo: Dona File

Fall Protection in Construction

U.S. Department of Labor
Occupational Safety and Health Administration

OSHA 3146-05R 2015

U.S. Department of Labor

Contents

The Continuing Need for Fall Protection

Why Does OSHA Have a Standard for Fall Protection?

Historically, falls are the leading cause of fatalities in construction, accounting for about one-third of all fatalities in the industry. For example, the Bureau of Labor Statistics reported that there were 291 fatal falls to a lower level in construction in 2013, out of 828 total fatalities.

OSHA recognizes that incidents involving falls are generally complex events, frequently involving a variety of factors. Consequently, the standard for fall protection deals with both the human and equipment-related issues in protecting workers from fall hazards. This publication is intended to help workers and employers better understand the Fall Protection in Construction standard's requirements and the reasons behind them.

What Subpart M – Fall Protection Covers

What is Subpart M?

Subpart M lays out the requirements and criteria for fall protection in construction workplaces. For example, it applies when workers are working at heights of 6 feet or more above a lower level. It also covers protection from falling objects, falls from tripping over or falling through holes, and protection when walking and working around dangerous equipment without regard to height. Subpart M provisions do not apply, however, to workers inspecting, investigating, or assessing workplace conditions prior to the actual start of work or after all construction work has been completed. The provisions of Subpart M can be found in Title 29 Code of Federal Regulations (CFR) Subpart M - Fall Protection, 29 CFR 1926.500, 29 CFR 1926.501, 29 CFR 1926.502, and 29 CFR 1926.503.

What are Employers' Responsibilities to provide Fall Protection?

Initially, employers must assess the workplace to determine if walking or working surfaces have the necessary strength and structural integrity to safely support the workers. Once it is determined that the work surfaces will safely support the work activity, the employer must determine whether fall protection is required (using the requirements set forth in 29 CFR 1926.501) and, if so, select and provide workers with fall protection systems that comply with the criteria found in 29 CFR 1926.502.

When must employers provide Fall Protection? The 6-foot rule.

Subpart M requires the use of fall protection when construction workers are working at heights of 6 feet or greater above a lower level. It applies at heights of less than 6 feet when working near dangerous equipment, for example, working over machinery with open drive belts, pulleys or gears or open vats of degreasing agents or acid.

What construction areas and activities does Subpart M cover?

The standard identifies certain areas and activities where fall protection or falling object protection may be needed. For example, it might require fall protection for a worker who is: on a ramp, runway, or another walkway; at the edge of an excavation; in a hoist area; on a steep roof; on, at, above, or near wall openings; on a walking or working surface with holes (including skylights) or unprotected sides or edges; above dangerous equipment; above a lower level where leading edges are under construction; on the face of formwork and reinforcing steel; or otherwise on a walking or working surface 6 feet or more above a lower level. The standard may also require fall protection where a worker is: constructing a leading edge; performing overhand bricklaying and related work; or engaged in roofing work on low-slope roofs, precast concrete erection, or residential construction. In addition, the standard requires falling object protection when a worker is exposed to falling objects.

What kinds of Fall Protection should employers use?

Generally, fall protection can be provided through the use of guardrail systems, safety net systems, or personal fall arrest systems. OSHA refers to these systems as conventional fall protection. Other systems and methods of fall protection may be used when performing certain activities. For example, when working on formwork, a positioning device system could be used. OSHA encourages employers to select systems that prevent falls of any kind, such as guardrails designed to keep workers from falling over the edge of a building.

Examples of Fall Protection Requirements for Certain Construction Activities

Leading Edges – 29 CFR 1926.501(b)(2)

Each worker constructing a leading edge 6 feet or more above a lower level must be protected by guardrail systems, safety net systems, or personal fall arrest systems. 29 CFR 1926.501(b)(2)(i).

Exception: When the employer can demonstrate that it is infeasible or creates a greater hazard to use these systems, the employer must develop and implement a fall protection plan which meets the requirements of 29 CFR 1926.502(k). See the section below on Fall Protection Plans.

Workers must be protected by guardrail systems, safety net systems, or personal fall arrest systems, *even if they are not engaged in leading edge work*, if they are on a walking or working surface that is 6 feet or more above a level where leading edges are under construction. 29 CFR 1926.501(b)(2)(ii).

Overhand Bricklaying and Related Work – 29 CFR 1926.501(b)(9)

When workers perform overhand bricklaying and related work 6 feet or more above a lower level:

- They must be protected by guardrail systems, safety net systems, or personal fall arrest systems, or
- They must work in a **controlled access zone (CAZ)**.

All workers reaching <u>more</u> than 10 inches below the level of the walking or working surface on which they are working must be protected by a guardrail system, safety net system, or personal fall arrest system.

Roofing Work on Low-Slope Roofs – 29 CFR 1926.501(b)(10)

A low-slope roof has a slope less than or equal to 4 in 12 (vertical to horizontal). When engaged in roofing work on a low-slope roof that has one or more unprotected side or edge 6 feet or more above lower levels, workers must be protected from falling by:

- Guardrail systems,
- Safety net systems,
- Personal fall arrest systems,
- A combination of conventional fall protection systems and warning line systems, or
- A warning line system and a safety monitoring system.

When engaged in roofing work on low-slope roofs 50 feet or less in width, the use of a safety monitoring system without a warning line system is permitted.

Working on Steep Roofs – 29 CFR 1926.501(b)(11)

A steep roof has a slope greater than 4 in 12 (vertical to horizontal). When working on a steep roof that has one or more unprotected side or edge 6 feet or more above lower levels, each worker must be protected by:

- Guardrail systems with toeboards,
- Safety net systems, or
- Personal fall arrest systems.

Residential Construction – 29 CFR 1926.501(b)(13)

Workers engaged in residential construction 6 feet or more above lower levels must be protected by conventional fall protection (i.e., guardrail systems, safety net systems, or personal fall arrest systems) unless another provision in 29 CFR 1926.501(b) provides for an alternative fall protection measure.

Exception: When the employer can demonstrate that it is infeasible or creates a greater hazard to use these systems, the employer must develop and implement a site-specific fall protection plan which meets the requirements of 29 CFR 1926.502(k). See the section on Fall Protection Plans, below.

Note: For purposes of determining the applicability of section 1926.501(b)(13), the term "residential construction" is interpreted as covering construction work that satisfies the following two elements: (1) the end-use of the structure being built must be as a home, i.e., a dwelling; and (2) the structure being built must be constructed using traditional wood frame construction materials and methods. The limited use of structural steel in a predominantly wood-framed home, such as a steel I-beam to help support wood framing, does not disqualify a structure from being considered residential construction. For more information see OSHA's Compliance Guidance for Residential Construction, STD 03-11-002.

Other Walking or Working Surfaces – 29 CFR 1926.501(b)(15)

As a general matter, each worker on a walking or working surface 6 feet or more above a lower level must be protected from falling by a guardrail system, a safety net system, or a personal fall arrest system.

Exceptions: For exceptions to this rule that specify different requirements, see 29 CFR 1926.500(a)(2) and 29 CFR 1926.501(b)(1) through (b)(14).

Conventional Fall Protection Systems

Guardrail Systems – 29 CFR 1926.502(b)

Guardrail systems are barriers erected to prevent workers from falling to lower levels. If the employer chooses to use guardrail systems to protect workers from falls, the following provisions apply:

- Top rails, or equivalent guardrail system members, must be 42 inches plus or minus 3 inches above the walking or working level. When workers are using stilts, the top edge of the top rail, or equivalent member, must be increased an amount equal to the height of the stilts. 29 CFR 1926.502(b)(1).

- Screens, midrails, mesh, intermediate vertical members, or equivalent intermediate structural members must be installed between the top edge of the guardrail system and the walking or working surface when there are no walls or parapet walls at least 21 inches high. 29 CFR 1926.502(b)(2).

- When midrails are used, they must be installed at a height midway between the top edge of the guardrail system and the walking or working level. 29 CFR 1926.502(b)(2)(i).

Properly installed guardrail system.

- When screens and mesh are used, they must extend from the top rail to the walking or working level and along the entire opening between top rail supports. 29 CFR 1926.502(b)(2)(ii). When necessary, screens and/or mesh must be installed in a manner to prevent a worker from falling underneath.

- When intermediate members (such as balusters) are used between posts, they must not be more than 19 inches apart. 29 CFR 1926.502(b)(2)(iii).

- Other structural members (such as additional midrails and architectural panels) must be installed so that there are no openings in the guardrail system more than 19 inches wide. 29 CFR 1926.502(b)(2)(iv).

- Guardrail systems must be capable of withstanding a force of at least 200 pounds applied within 2 inches of the top edge, in any outward or downward direction, at any point along the top edge. 29 CFR 1926.502(b)(3).

- Midrails, screens, mesh, intermediate vertical members, solid panels, and equivalent structural members must be capable of withstanding a force of at least 150 pounds applied in any downward or outward direction at any point along the midrail or other member. 29 CFR 1926.502(b)(5).

- Guardrail systems must have a surface to protect workers from punctures or lacerations and to prevent clothing from snagging. 29 CFR 1926.502(b)(6).

- The ends of top rails and midrails must not overhang terminal posts, except where an overhang poses no projection hazard. 29 CFR 1926.502(b)(7).

- Steel and plastic banding cannot be used as top rails or midrails. 29 CFR 1926.502(b)(8).

- Top rails and midrails of guardrail systems must have a nominal diameter or thickness of at least 1/4 inch to prevent cuts and lacerations. 29 CFR 1926.502(b)(9).

- If wire rope is used for top rails, it must be flagged at not more than 6-foot intervals with high-visibility material. 29 CFR 1926.502(b)(9).

- When guardrail systems are used at hoisting areas, a chain, gate, or removable guardrail section must be placed across the access opening between guardrail sections during those times when hoisting operations are not taking place. 29 CFR 1926.502(b)(10).

- When guardrail systems are used at holes, they must be set up on all unprotected sides or edges. When a hole is used for the passage of materials, it must not have more than two sides with removable guardrail sections. When the hole is not in use, it must be covered or provided with a guardrail system along all unprotected sides or edges. 29 CFR 1926.502(b)(11) & (12).

■ If guardrail systems are used around holes being used as access points (such as ladderways), gates must be used. Alternatively, the point of access must be offset to prevent workers from accidentally walking straight into the hole. 29 CFR 1926.502(b)(13).

■ If guardrails are used on ramps and runways, they must be erected on each unprotected side or edge. 29 CFR 1926.502(b)(14).

■ Manila, plastic, or synthetic rope used for top rails or midrails must be inspected as frequently as necessary to ensure its strength and stability. 29 CFR 1926.502(b)(15).

Safety Net Systems – 29 CFR 1926.502(c)

When safety nets are used, they must be installed as close as practicable under the walking or working surface on which workers are working and never more than 30 feet below that level. 29 CFR 1926.502(c)(1). When nets are used on bridges, the potential fall area from the walking or working surface to the net must be unobstructed. 29 CFR 1926.502(c)(1). All safety nets must be installed with sufficient clearance underneath to prevent a falling body from hitting the surface or structure below the net. 29 CFR 1926.502(c)(3). If the employer chooses to use nets, the following criteria apply:

Vertical distance from a working level to the horizontal plane of the net	Minimum required horizontal distance from the edge of a working surface to the outer edge of the net
Up to 5 feet	8 feet
More than 5 feet up to 10 feet	10 feet
More than 10 feet	13 feet

Drop-testing is required to ensure that safety nets and safety net installations are working properly. See 29 CFR 1926.502(c)(4)(i) for more details. If an employer can demonstrate that it is unreasonable to perform a drop-test, then the employer or a designated competent person must certify that the net and its installation is in compliance with the standard. See 29 CFR 1926.502(c)(4)(ii) for more details on certification and certification records.

Safety nets used in construction sites.

- Do not use defective nets. Inspect nets at least once a week for wear, damage, or deterioration of components such as net connection points. 29 CFR 1926.502(c)(5).

- Remove materials, tools, and other items as soon as possible from the net and at least before the next work shift. 29 CFR 1926.502(c)(6).

- To work properly, a safety net must have safe openings. Mesh openings must not exceed 36 square inches, and must not be longer than 6 inches on any side. Each opening, measured center-to-center of mesh ropes or webbing, must not exceed 6 inches. 29 CFR 1926.502(c)(7).

- All mesh crossings must be secured to prevent the openings from enlarging. 29 CFR 1926.502(c)(7).

- Use safety net (or section of net) with a border rope possessing a minimum breaking strength of 5,000 pounds. 29 CFR 1926.502(c)(8).

- Do not allow one weak link to compromise a safety net. Use connections between safety net panels that are as strong as integral net components and spaced no more than 6 inches apart. 29 CFR 1926.502(c)(9).

Personal Fall Arrest Systems – 29 CFR 1926.502(d)

A personal fall arrest system is a system used to safely stop (arrest) a worker who is falling from a working level. It consists of an anchorage, connectors, and a body harness. It also may include a lanyard, deceleration device, lifeline, or suitable combinations of these. Under Subpart M, body belts (safety belts) **are prohibited** for use as part of a personal fall arrest system.*

When employers choose to use a personal fall arrest system as a means of worker fall protection they must:

- Limit the maximum arresting force on a worker to 1,800 pounds when used with a body harness. 29 CFR 1926.502(d)(16)(ii).

Know the A, B, Cs of Personal Fall Arrest Systems

Anchorages

Body harness

Components (connectors like snaphooks or Dee-rings, connection points, lanyards, deceleration devices, lifelines, etc.)

- Be rigged so that a worker can neither free fall more than 6 feet nor contact any lower level. 29 CFR 926.502(d)(16)(iii).

- Bring a worker to a complete stop and limit the maximum deceleration distance a worker travels to 3.5 feet. 29 CFR 1926.502(d)(16)(iv).

- Have sufficient strength to withstand twice the potential impact energy of a worker free falling a distance of 6 feet or the free fall distance permitted by the system, whichever is less. 29 CFR 1926.502(d)(16)(v).

- Be inspected prior to each use for wear, damage, and other deterioration. Defective components must be removed from service. 29 CFR 1926.502(d)(21).

*Note: Limited use of body belts (safety belts) can still be used as part of a positioning device system or fall restraint system See more information under Positioning Device Systems and Fall Restraint Systems, below.

Personal Fall Arrest System Components

Snaphooks

- Snaphooks must be the locking type and designed and used to prevent disengagement from any component part of the personal fall arrest system. 29 CFR 1926.502(d)(5).

- Locking type snaphooks may also be used when designed for the following connections:
  - directly to webbing, rope, or wire rope;
  - to each other;
  - to a Dee-ring to which another snaphook or other connector is attached;
  - to a horizontal lifeline; or
  - to any object which is incompatibly shaped or dimensioned in relation to the snaphook, such that unintentional disengagement could occur by the connected object being able to depress the snaphook keeper and release itself. 29 CFR 1926.502(d)(6).

Horizontal Lifelines

- On suspended scaffolds or similar work platforms with horizontal lifelines that may become vertical lifelines, the devices used to connect to a horizontal lifeline must be capable of locking in both directions on the lifeline. 29 CFR 1926.502(d)(7).

- Horizontal lifelines must be designed, installed, and used under the supervision of a qualified person, as part of a complete personal fall arrest system that maintains a safety factor of at least two. 29 CFR 1926.502(d)(8).

Vertical Lifelines and Lanyards

■ Vertical lifelines and lanyards must have a minimum breaking strength of 5,000 pounds. 29 CFR 1926.502(d)(9).

■ Lifelines must be protected against being cut or abraded. 29 CFR 1926.502(d)(11).

Self-retracting Lifelines and Lanyards

■ Self-retracting lifelines and lanyards that automatically limit free fall distance to 2 feet or less must be capable of sustaining a minimum tensile load of 3,000 pounds applied to the device with the lifeline or lanyard in the fully extended position. 29 CFR 1926.502(d)(12).

■ Self-retracting lifelines and lanyards which do not limit free fall distance to 2 feet or less, ripstitch lanyards, and tearing and deforming lanyards must be capable of sustaining a minimum tensile load of 5,000 pounds applied to the device with the lifeline or lanyard in the fully extended position. 29 CFR 1926.502(d)(13).

Ropes and Straps

■ Ropes and straps (webbing) used in lanyards, lifelines, and strength components of body belts and body harnesses must be made of synthetic fibers. 29 CFR 1926.502(d)(14).

Anchorages

■ Anchorages used to attach personal fall arrest systems must be designed, installed, and used under the supervision of a qualified person, as part of a complete personal fall arrest system which maintains a safety factor of at least two. Alternatively, the anchorages must be independent of any anchorage being used to support or suspend platforms and must be capable of supporting at least 5,000 pounds per worker attached or be capable of supporting at least twice the expected impact load. 29 CFR 1926.502(d)(15).

Positioning Device Systems – 29 CFR 1926.502(e)

OSHA defines a positioning device system as a body belt or body harness system rigged to allow a worker to be supported on an elevated vertical surface, such as a wall, and work with both hands free while leaning.

- Body belt or body harness systems are to be set up so that a worker can free fall no farther than 2 feet. 29 CFR 1926.502(e)(1).
- Body belts or harnesses must be secured to an anchorage capable of supporting at least twice the potential impact load of a worker's fall or 3,000 pounds, whichever is greater. 29 CFR 1926.502(e)(2).

Positioning Device System Components

Snaphooks, Dee-rings, and Other Connectors

Requirements for components are similar or identical to provisions relating to Personal Fall Arrest System components found in 29 CFR 1926.502(d).

For strength and safe use requirements of snaphooks, Dee-rings, and other connectors when used with positioning device systems, see 29 CFR 1926.502(e)(3) through (10).

Fall Restraint Systems

While fall restraint systems are not mentioned in Subpart M, OSHA recognizes a fall restraint system as a means of prevention. The system, if properly used, tethers a worker in a manner that **will not allow a fall of any distance**. This system is comprised of a body belt or body harness, an anchorage, connectors, and other necessary equipment. Other components typically include

Photo: Skip Pennington

a lanyard, a lifeline, and other devices. For a restraint system to work, the anchorage must be strong enough to prevent the worker from moving past the point where the system is fully extended, including an appropriate safety factor.

In a November 2, 1995 interpretation letter to Mr. Dennis Gilmore, OSHA suggested that, at a minimum, a fall restraint system must have the capacity to withstand at least 3,000 pounds or twice the maximum expected force that is needed to restrain the person from exposure to the fall hazard. In determining this force, consideration should be given to site-specific factors such as the force generated by a person (including his/her tools, equipment, and materials) walking, slipping, tripping, leaning, or sliding along the work surface.

Letters of Interpretation

There are a number of Letters of Interpretation pertinent to fall protection that may affect your operation. OSHA Letters of Interpretation do not create new or additional requirements but rather explain these requirements and how they apply to particular circumstances. The letters constitute OSHA's interpretation of the requirements discussed. From time to time, letters are affected when the Agency updates a standard, a legal decision impacts a standard, or changes in technology affect the interpretation. To assure that you are using the correct information and guidance, please consult OSHA's website at www.osha.gov. If you have further questions, contact the Directorate of Construction at (202) 693-2020.

Additional Fall Protection Systems

Warning Line Systems – 29 CFR 1926.502(f)

OSHA defines a warning line system as a barrier erected on a roof to warn workers that they are approaching an unprotected roof side or edge, and to designate an area in which roofing work may take place without the use of guardrails, body harnesses, or safety net systems to protect workers in the area. Warning line systems consist of ropes, wires, or chains, plus supporting stanchions. If an employer chooses to use warning line systems, the following provisions apply:

- The warning line must be erected around all sides of roof work areas. 29 CFR 1926.502(f)(1).
- When mechanical equipment is not being used, the warning line must be erected at least 6 feet from the roof edge. 29 CFR 1926.502(f)(1)(i).
- When mechanical equipment is being used the warning line must be erected:
  - At least 6 feet from the roof edge parallel to the direction of mechanical equipment operation; and
  - At least 10 feet from the roof edge perpendicular to the direction of mechanical equipment operation. 29 CFR 1926.502(f)(1)(ii).
- The rope, wire, or chain must be flagged at not more than 6-foot intervals with high-visibility material. 29 CFR 1926.502(f)(2)(i).
- The rope, wire, or chain must be rigged and supported so that:
  - The lowest point (including sag) is at least 34 inches from the walking or working surface; and
  - Its highest point is no more than 39 inches from the walking or working surface. 29 CFR 1926.502(f)(2)(ii).
- Stanchions, after being rigged with warning lines, must be capable of resisting, without tipping over, a force of at least 16 pounds applied horizontally against the stanchion, 30 inches above the walking or working surface, perpendicular to the warning line and in the direction of the floor, roof, or platform edge. 29 CFR 1926.502(f)(2)(iii).
- The rope, wire, or chain must have a minimum tensile strength of 500 pounds. After being attached to the stanchions, it must support, without breaking, the loads applied to the stanchions as prescribed in 29 CFR 1926.502(f)(2)(iii) & 29 CFR 1926.502(f)(2)(iv).

- The rope, wire, or chain must be attached to each stanchion in such a way that pulling on one section of the line between stanchions will not result in slack being taken up in the adjacent section before the stanchion tips over. 29 CFR 1926.502(f)(2)(v).

Controlled Access Zones – 29 CFR 1926.502(g)

- A controlled access zone is a work area in which certain types of work may take place without using conventional fall protection systems. Worker access to these areas must be carefully controlled. For example, a controlled access zone would be designated where overhand bricklaying was occurring without the protection of guardrails. In this example, only masons and other workers actually engaged in the bricklaying would be allowed in the controlled access zone.

- When used to control access to areas where leading edge and other operations are taking place, the controlled access zones must be defined by a control line or by any other means that restricts access. 29 CFR 1926.502(g)(1).

- When control lines are used to define a controlled access zone, they must be erected at least 6 feet and no more than 25 feet from the unprotected or leading edge, except when precast concrete members are being erected. In the latter case, the control line is to be erected at least 6 feet and no more than 60 feet or half the length of the member being erected, whichever is less, from the leading edge. 29 CFR 1926.502(g)(1)(i) and (ii).

- The control line must extend along the entire length of and approximately parallel to the unprotected side or leading edge and be connected on each side to a guardrail system or wall. 29 CFR 1926.502(g)(1)(iii) and (iv).

- When controlled access zones are used to limit access to areas where overhand bricklaying and related work are taking place:
  - A control line must be erected to define the work zone and must be erected at least 10 feet and no more than 15 feet from the working edge. 29 CFR 1926.502(g)(2)(i).

The control lines must be erected approximately parallel to the working edge and must extend for a distance sufficient to enclose all workers performing overhand bricklaying and related work at the working edge. 29 CFR 1926.502(g)(2)(ii).

- Additional control lines must be erected at each end of the controlled access zone to enclose the work area. 29 CFR 1926.502(g)(2)(iii).

- Only workers engaged in overhand bricklaying or related work are permitted in the controlled access zone. 29 CFR 1926.502(g)(2)(iv).

▪ Control lines must consist of ropes, wires, tapes, or equivalent materials, and supporting stanchions. When used, each control line must:

- Be flagged or otherwise clearly marked at not more than 6-foot intervals with high-visibility material. 29 CFR 1926.502(g)(3)(i).

- Be rigged and supported in such a way that the lowest point (including sag) is not less than 39 inches from the walking or working surface; and the highest point is not more than 45 inches, or more than 50 inches when overhand bricklaying operations are being performed, from the walking or working surface. 29 CFR 1926.502(g)(3)(ii).

- Have a breaking strength of at least 200 pounds. 29 CFR 1926.502(g)(3)(iii).

▪ On floors and roofs where guardrail systems are not in place prior to the beginning of overhand bricklaying operations, controlled access zones must be enlarged as necessary to enclose all points of access, material handling areas, and storage areas. 29 CFR 1926.502(g)(4).

▪ On floors and roofs where guardrail systems are in place but need to be removed to allow overhand bricklaying work or leading edge work to take place, only that portion of the guardrail necessary to accomplish that day's work is allowed to be removed. 29 CFR 1926.502(g)(5).

Safety Monitoring Systems – 29 CFR 1926.502(h)

A safety monitoring system is an alternative fall protection option for low-slope roofing work under 29 CFR 1926.501(b)(10). If employers elect to use a safety monitoring system, they must designate a competent person to monitor the safety of workers and to warn them when their work puts them close to a fall hazard.

The safety monitor must:

- Be competent in the recognition of fall hazards. 29 CFR 1926.502(h)(1)(i);
- Warn workers when it appears that they are unaware of fall hazards or when the workers are acting in an unsafe manner. 29 CFR 1926.502(h)(1)(ii);
- Be on the same walking or working surfaces as the workers and be able to see them. 29 CFR 1926.502(h)(1)(iii);
- Be close enough to the work operations to speak directly with workers. 29 CFR 1926.502(h)(1)(iv); and
- Have no other duties to distract them from their monitoring function. 29 CFR 1926.502(h)(1)(v).

Employers must ensure that:

- Mechanical equipment is not used or stored in areas where safety monitoring systems are being used to monitor workers engaged in roofing operations on low-slope roofs. 29 CFR 1926.502(h)(2);
- No worker, other than one engaged in roofing work on low-slope roofs or one covered by a fall protection plan, enters an area where a worker is being protected by a safety monitoring system. 29 CFR 1926.502(h)(3); and
- All workers in a controlled access zone have been instructed to promptly comply with fall hazard warnings issued by safety monitors. 29 CFR 1926.502(h)(4).

Safety monitoring systems must also be used as part of a fall protection plan under 29 CFR 1926.502(k), where no other alternative measure has been implemented. As explained in more detail below, the use of a fall protection plan is limited to residential construction work, precast concrete work, and leading edge work (see 29 CFR 1926.501(b)(2), (b)(12) and (b)(13)). The employer must first demonstrate that it is infeasible or creates a greater hazard to use conventional fall protection equipment.

Other Hazards that Require Fall Protection

A construction environment poses many hazards requiring protection. Below are some fall hazards that cannot be overlooked.

Hoist Areas – 29 CFR 1926.501(b)(3)

Each worker in a hoist area must be protected from falling 6 feet or more by guardrail systems or personal fall arrest systems. There may be times when the guardrail systems (or chain, gate, or guardrail) must be removed in whole or part to facilitate hoisting operations. For example, during the landing of materials, a worker may need to lean through the access opening or out over the edge of the access opening to receive or guide equipment and materials. At such times a personal fall arrest system must be used to protect the worker from falling through the unprotected opening.

Holes – 29 CFR 1926.501(b)(4)

- Each worker on walking or working surfaces must be protected from falling through holes (including skylights) that are more than 6 feet above lower levels, by personal fall arrest systems, covers, or guardrail systems erected around such holes. 29 CFR 1926.501(b)(4)(i).

- Each worker on a walking or working surface must be protected from tripping in or stepping into or through holes (including skylights) by covers. 29 CFR 1926.501(b)(4)(ii).

Covered floor hole marked, and with a guardrail surrounding it.

Ramps, Runways, and Other Walkways – 29 CFR 1926.501(b)(6)

Each worker on a ramp, runway, or other walkway must be protected by guardrail systems against falling 6 feet or more.

Excavations – 29 CFR 1926.501(b)(7)

- Each worker at the edge of an excavation 6 feet or more deep must be protected from falling by guardrail systems, fences, or barricades when the excavation cannot be readily seen because of plant growth or other visual barrier. 29 CFR 1926.501(b)(7)(i).

- Each worker at the edge of a well, pit, shaft, and similar excavation 6 feet or more deep must be protected from falling by guardrail systems, fences, or barricades, or covers. 29 CFR 1926.502(b)(7)(ii).

Dangerous Equipment – 29 CFR 1926.501(b)(8)

- When working 6 feet or more above dangerous equipment, each worker must be protected by guardrail systems, safety net systems, or personal fall arrest systems. 29 CFR 1926.502(b)(8)(ii).

- When working less than 6 feet above dangerous equipment, each worker must be protected from falling into or onto the dangerous equipment by a guardrail system or equipment guards. 29 CFR 1926.502(b)(8)(i).

Wall Openings – 29 CFR 1926.501(b)(14)

Each worker working on, at, above, or near wall openings (including those with chutes attached), where the outside bottom edge of the wall opening is 6 feet or more above lower levels and the inside bottom edge of the wall opening is less than 39 inches above the walking or working surface, must be protected with a guardrail system, a safety net system, or a personal fall arrest system.

Protection from Falling Objects

Falling objects can also pose a hazard to workers. Falling object protection must comply with the following provisions:

Guardrails – 29 CFR 1926.502(j)(5)

When guardrail systems are used to prevent materials from falling from one level to another, any openings must be small enough to prevent passage of falling objects.

Overhand Bricklaying and Related Work – 29 CFR 1926.502(j)(6)

During overhand bricklaying and related work, no materials or equipment except masonry and mortar may be stored within 4 feet of working edges. Excess mortar, broken or scattered masonry units, and all other materials and debris must be kept clear of the working area by removal at regular intervals.

Roofing Work – 29 CFR 1926.502(j)(7)

During roofing work, materials and equipment must not be stored within 6 feet of a roof edge unless guardrail systems are erected at the edge. Any materials piled, grouped, or stacked near a roof edge must be stable and self-supporting.

Toeboards – 29 CFR 1926.502(j)(1) through (4)

When toeboards are used as protection from falling objects, they must be erected along the edges of the overhead walking or working surface for a distance sufficient to protect workers working below. 29 CFR 1926.502(j)(1). Other criteria include:

- Toeboards must be capable of withstanding, without failure, a force of at least 50 pounds applied in any downward or outward direction at any point along the toeboard. 29 CFR 1926.502(j)(2).
- Toeboards must be at least 3.5 inches tall from their top edge to the level of the walking or working surface, must have no

more than 0.25 inch clearance above the walking or working surface, and must be solid or have openings no larger than one inch in its greatest dimension. 29 CFR 1926.502(j)(3).

- Where tools, equipment, or materials are piled higher than the top edge of a toeboard, paneling or screening must be erected from the walking or working surface or toeboard to the top of a guardrail system's top rail or midrail, for a distance sufficient to protect workers below. 29 CFR 1926.502(j)(4).

Canopies – 29 CFR 1926.502(j)(8)

When used as protection from falling objects, canopies must be strong enough to prevent collapse and to prevent penetration by any objects that may fall onto them.

Fall Protection Plans

Presumption of Feasibility

As a general matter, OSHA presumes that using conventional fall protection (that is, guardrails, personal fall arrest systems, or safety nets) is feasible and will not create a greater hazard to use. However, as outlined below, there are a few circumstances when an employer can use a site-specifc fall protection plan instead of conventional fall protection.

When Can I Use a Fall Protection Plan?

It is possible that during leading edge work (29 CFR 1926.501(b)(2)), precast concrete erection (29 CFR 1926.501(b)(12)), or residential construction (29 CFR 1926.501(b)(13)), it may be infeasible or may create a greater hazard to use conventional fall protection for a specific task. In those circumstances, employers may implement a fall protection plan that complies with 29 CFR 1926.502(k).

> IMPORTANT: The employer has the burden of establishing that it is appropriate to implement a fall protection plan instead of implementing conventional fall protection systems.

Elements of a Fall Protection Plan – 29 CFR 1926.502(k)

▪ A fall protection plan must be prepared by a qualified person and developed specifically for the site where the work is being performed. 29 CFR 1926.502(k)(1).

▪ The fall protection plan must be maintained and kept up to date. 29 CFR 1926.502(k)(1).

▪ Any changes to the fall protection plan must be approved by a qualified person. 29 CFR 1926.502(k)(2).

▪ A copy of the fall protection plan with all approved changes must be maintained at the job site. 29 CFR 1926.502(k)(3).

▪ A competent person must supervise the implementation of the fall protection plan. 29 CFR 1926.502(k)(4).

▪ The plan must document the reasons why the use of conventional fall protection is infeasible or would create a greater hazard. 29 CFR 1926.502(k)(5).

▪ The plan must include a written discussion of other measures that will be taken to reduce or eliminate the fall hazard for workers who cannot be provided with protection using conventional fall protection systems. For example, the employer must discuss the extent to which scaffolds, ladders, or vehicle-mounted work platforms can be used to provide a safer working surface and thereby reduce the hazard of falling. 29 CFR 1926.502(k)(6).

▪ The plan must identify each location where conventional fall protection methods cannot be used. These locations must then be classified as controlled access zones, and the employer must comply with the criteria in 29 CFR 1926.502(g) and 29 CFR 1926.502(k)(7).

▪ Where no other alternative measure has been implemented, the employer must implement a safety monitoring system that complies with 29 CFR 1926.502(h) and 29 CFR 1926.502(k)(8).

▪ The plan must include a statement which provides the name or other method of identification for each worker who is authorized to work in controlled access zones. No other workers may enter controlled access zones. 29 CFR 1926.502(k)(9).

- In the event that a worker falls, or some other related, serious incident occurs (for example, a near miss), the employer must investigate the circumstances to determine if the fall protection plan needs to be changed. For example, the plan may need to add new practices, procedures, or training. The employer must implement the needed changes to prevent similar types of falls or incidents. 29 CFR 1926.502(k)(10).

Fall Protection Training

Requirements – 29 CFR 1926.503

Employers must provide a fall protection training program to workers who might be exposed to fall hazards. Training must include how to recognize fall hazards and how to minimize them. 29 CFR 1926.503(a)(1).

The employer must assure that each worker has been trained as necessary, by a competent person who is qualified in the following areas:

- The nature of fall hazards in the work area. 29 CFR 1926.503(a)(2)(i).
- The correct procedures for erecting, maintaining, disassembling, and inspecting the fall protection systems to be used. 29 CFR 1926.503(a)(2)(ii).
- The use and operation of controlled access zones; guardrail, personal fall arrest, safety net, warning line, and safety monitoring systems; and other protection to be used. 29 CFR 1926.503(a)(2)(iii).
- The role of each worker in the safety monitoring system when the system is used. 29 CFR 1926.503(a)(2)(iv).
- The limitations on the use of mechanical equipment during the performance of roofing work on low-slope roofs. 29 CFR 1926.503(a)(2)(v).
- The correct procedures for equipment and materials handling and storage and the erection of overhead protection. 29 CFR 1926.503(a)(2)(vi).

- The role of workers in fall protection plans. 29 CFR 1926.503(a)(2)(vii).
- OSHA's fall protection requirements, published as Subpart M. 29 CFR 1926.503(a)(2)(viii).

Verification of Training

Employers must verify worker training by preparing a <u>written</u> certification record. The record must contain the name or other identity of the worker trained, the dates of the training, and the signature of either the person who conducted the training or the employer. 29 CFR 1926.503(b)(1).

When an employer has reason to believe that an affected worker does not recognize existing fall hazards at some point after the initial training, the employer is required to provide retraining for that worker. For example, workers must be retrained when:

- Changes in the workplace render previous training obsolete. 29 CFR 1926.503(c)(1).
- Fall protection equipment or systems have changed. 29 CFR 1926.503(c)(2).
- Inadequacies in workers' knowledge or use of fall protection systems or equipment indicate that they have not adequately understood or retained previous training. 29 CFR 1926.503(c)(3).

Fall Protection Requirements in Other OSHA Construction Standards

Other OSHA construction standards also contain fall protection requirements. Employers covered by another standard may have to comply with the requirements in the other standard and those in Subpart M, unless one of the exceptions listed in 29 CFR 1926.500(a)(2), 1926.500(a)(3), or 1926.500(a)(4) applies. OSHA included these exceptions because other means of providing fall protection (for example, when using ladders and scaffolds) may eliminate the need for providing fall protection under Subpart M. For example, employers with workers engaged in the construction of electric transmission or distribution lines or equipment should refer to Subpart V – Power Transmission and Distribution for specific fall protection requirements. However, employers should be aware that their workers are still covered by Subpart M when the workers are engaged in activities not covered by Subpart V or another of the exceptions under 29 CFR 1926.500.

The following subparts of OSHA's Construction standards address fall protection requirements and performance criteria outside of Subpart M:

- Personal Protective and Life Saving Equipment – Subpart E (applies to belts, lanyards, lifelines, nets for work on tanks, communication and broadcast towers);
- Scaffolds – Subpart L;
- Steel Erection – Subpart R;
- Underground Construction, Caissons, Cofferdams, and Compressed Air – Subpart S (applies to certain types of equipment in tunneling operations);
- Power Transmission and Distribution – Subpart V;
- Stairways and Ladders – Subpart X; and
- Cranes and Derricks in Construction – Subpart CC.

Subpart M – Fall Protection: Non-mandatory Appendices

Appendix A to Subpart M – Determining Roof Widths – Non-mandatory Guidelines for Complying with 1926.501(b)(10)

This appendix serves as a guideline to help employers comply with the requirements of 1926.501(b)(10). Section 1926.501(b)(10) allows the use of a safety monitoring system alone as a means of providing fall protection during the performance of roofing operations on low-sloped roofs 50 feet (15.25 m) or less in width.

Appendix B to Subpart M – Guardrail Systems – Non-mandatory Guidelines for Complying with 1926.502(b)

This appendix serves as a guideline to assist employers in designing and building guardrail systems in compliance with 1926.502(b)(3), (4), and (5).

Appendix C to Subpart M – Personal Fall Arrest Systems – Non-mandatory Guidelines for Complying with 1926.502(d) This appendix serves as a non-mandatory guideline to help employers comply with the requirements in 1926.502(d). Section I, paragraphs (b), (c), (d) and (e) describe methods for testing personal fall arrest systems and positioning device systems.

Appendix D to Subpart M – Positioning Device Systems – Non-mandatory Guidelines for Complying with 1926.502(e) This appendix serves as a non-mandatory guideline to help employers comply with the requirements for positioning device systems in 1926.502(e). The procedures listed here, along with those in Appendix C (above), describe methods for testing positioning device systems to comply with 1926.502(e) (3) and (4) of Subpart M.

Appendix E to Subpart M – Sample Fall Protection Plan – Non-mandatory Guidelines for Complying with 1926.502(k) This appendix provides sample fall protection plans for employers engaged in leading edge work, precast concrete construction, or residential construction work. The employer must be able to demonstrate that it is infeasible or creates a greater hazard to use conventional fall protection systems.

Definitions

The definitions in this section that affect Subpart M are found in 29 CFR 1926.32; 29 CFR 1926.500; and STD 03-11-002 Compliance Guidance for Residential Construction.

Anchorage – a secure point of attachment for lifelines, lanyards, or deceleration devices.

Body belt (safety belt) – a strap with means both for securing it about the waist and for attaching it to a lanyard, lifeline, or deceleration device. *Note: Since January 1, 1998, OSHA has prohibited the use of a body belt as part of a **personal fall arrest system**. Exception: When used correctly, body belts are recognized by OSHA as an acceptable fall protection component when used as a part of either a restraining device which prevents a fall or a positioning device which limits a free fall to 2 feet.*

Body harness – straps which may be secured about the worker in a manner that will distribute the fall arrest forces over at least the thighs, pelvis, waist, chest, and shoulders, with means for attaching it to other components of a personal fall arrest system.

Buckle – any device for holding the body belt or body harness closed around the worker's body.

Competent person – one who is capable of identifying existing and predictable hazards in the surroundings or working conditions which are unsanitary, hazardous, or dangerous to workers, and who has authorization to take prompt corrective measures to eliminate them.

Connector – a device which is used to couple (connect) parts of the personal fall arrest system and positioning device systems together. It may be an independent component of the system, such as a carabiner, or it may be an integral component of part of the system (such as a buckle or Dee-ring sewn into a body belt or body harness, or a snaphook spliced or sewn to a lanyard or self-retracting lanyard).

Controlled access zone (CAZ) – an area in which certain work (for example, overhand bricklaying) may take place without the use of guardrail systems, personal fall arrest systems, or safety net systems; and where access to the zone is controlled.

Dangerous equipment – equipment (such as pickling or galvanizing tanks, degreasing units, machinery, electrical equipment, and other units) which, as a result of form or function, may be hazardous to workers who fall onto or into such equipment.

Deceleration device – any mechanism (such as a rope grab, rip-stitch lanyard, specially-woven lanyard, tearing or deforming lanyards, automatic self-retracting lifelines/lanyards, etc.) which serves to dissipate a substantial amount of energy during a fall arrest, or otherwise limit the energy imposed on a worker during fall arrest.

Deceleration distance – the additional vertical distance a falling employee travels, excluding lifeline elongation and free fall distance, before stopping, from the point at which the deceleration device begins to operate. It is measured as the distance between the location of a worker's body belt or body harness attachment point at the moment of activation (at the onset of fall arrest forces) of the deceleration device during a fall, and the location of that attachment point after the worker comes to a full stop.

Equivalent – alternative designs, materials, or methods to protect against a hazard, which the employer can demonstrate will provide an equal or greater degree of safety for workers than the methods, materials, or designs specified in the standard.

Failure – load refusal, breakage, or separation of component parts. Load refusal is the point where the ultimate strength is exceeded.

Free fall – the act of falling before a personal fall arrest system begins to apply force to arrest the fall.

Free fall distance – the vertical displacement of the fall arrest attachment point on the worker's body belt or body harness between onset of the fall and just before the system begins to apply force to arrest the fall. This distance excludes deceleration distance and lifeline/lanyard elongation, but includes any deceleration device slide distance or self-retracting lifeline/lanyard extension before they operate and fall arrest forces occur.

Guardrail system – a barrier erected to prevent workers from falling to lower levels.

Hole – a gap or void 2 inches or more in its least dimension, in a floor, roof, or other walking or working surface.

Infeasible – impossible to perform the construction work using a conventional fall protection system (that is, guardrail system, safety net system, or personal fall arrest system); or technologically impossible to use any one of these systems to provide fall protection.

Lanyard – a flexible line of rope, wire rope, or strap which generally has a connector at each end for connecting the body belt or body harness to a deceleration device, lifeline, or anchorage.

Leading edge – the edge of a floor, roof, or formwork for a floor or other walking or working surface (such as the deck) which changes location as additional floor, roof, decking, or formwork sections are placed, formed, or constructed. A leading edge is considered to be an "unprotected side and edge" during periods when it is not actively and continuously under construction.

Lifeline – a component consisting of a flexible line for connection to an anchorage at one end to hang vertically (vertical lifeline), or for connection to anchorages at both ends to stretch horizontally (horizontal lifeline), and which serves as a means for connecting other components of a personal fall arrest system to the anchorage.

Low-slope roof – a roof having a slope less than or equal to 4 in 12 (vertical to horizontal).

Lower levels – those areas or surfaces to which a worker can fall. Such areas or surfaces include, but are not limited to, ground levels, floors, platforms, ramps, runways, excavations, pits, tanks, material, water, equipment, structures, or portions thereof.

Mechanical equipment – all motor- or human-propelled wheeled equipment used for roofing work, except wheelbarrows and mop carts.

Opening – a gap or void 30 inches or more high and 18 inches or more wide, in a wall or partition, through which workers can fall to a lower level.

Overhand bricklaying and related work – the process of laying bricks and masonry units such that the surface of the wall to be jointed is on the opposite side of the wall from the mason, requiring the mason to lean over the wall to complete the work. Related work includes mason tending and electrical installation incorporated into the brick wall during the overhand bricklaying process.

Personal fall arrest system – a system used to arrest a worker in a fall from a working level. It consists of an anchorage, connectors, and a body harness. It may include a lanyard, deceleration device, lifeline, or suitable combinations of these. *Note: Since January 1, 1998, the use of a body belt for fall arrest has been prohibited.*

Positioning device system – a body belt or body harness system rigged to allow a worker to be supported on an elevated vertical surface, such as a wall, and work with both hands free while leaning.

Qualified – one who, by possession of a recognized degree, certificate, or professional standing, or who by extensive knowledge, training, and experience, has successfully demonstrated his ability to solve or resolve problems relating to the subject matter, the work, or the project.

Rope grab – a deceleration device which travels on a lifeline and automatically, by friction, engages the lifeline and locks so as to arrest the fall of a worker. A rope grab usually employs the principles of inertial locking, cam/level locking, or both.

Roof – the exterior surface on the top of a building. This does not include floors or formwork which, because a building has not been completed, temporarily become the top surface of a building.

Roofing work – the hoisting, storage, application, and removal of roofing materials and equipment, including related insulation, sheet metal, and vapor barrier work, but not including the construction of the roof deck.

Safety-monitoring system – a safety system in which a competent person is responsible for recognizing and warning workers of fall hazards.

Self-retracting lifeline/lanyard – a deceleration device containing a drum-wound line which can be slowly extracted from, or retracted onto, the drum under slight tension during normal worker movement, and which, after onset of a fall, automatically locks the drum and arrests the fall.

Snaphook – a connector comprised of a hook-shaped member with a normally closed keeper, or similar arrangement, which may be opened to permit the hook to receive an object and, when released, automatically closes to retain the object. Snaphooks are generally one of two types:

(1) The *locking* type with a self-closing, self-locking keeper which remains closed and locked until unlocked and pressed open for connection or disconnection; or

(2) The *non-locking* type with a self-closing keeper which remains closed until pressed open for connection or disconnection. As of January 1, 1998, the use of a non-locking snaphook as part of personal fall arrest systems and positioning device systems is prohibited.

Steep roof – a roof having a slope greater than 4 in 12 (vertical to horizontal).

Toeboard – a low protective barrier that will prevent the fall of materials and equipment to lower levels and provide workers protection from falls.

Unprotected sides and edges – any side or edge (except at entrances to points of access) of a walking or working surface (for example, floor, roof, ramp, or runway) where there is no wall or guardrail system at least 39 inches high.

Walking/working (walking or working) surface – any surface (whether horizontal or vertical) on which a worker walks or works, including but not limited to floors, roofs, ramps, bridges, runways, formwork and concrete reinforcing steel; but not including ladders, vehicles, or trailers, on which workers must be located in order to perform their job duties.

Warning line system – a barrier erected on a roof to warn workers that they are approaching an unprotected roof side or edge, and which designates an area in which roofing work may take place without the use of guardrail, body harness, or safety net systems to protect workers in the area.

Work area – that portion of a walking or working surface where job duties are being performed.

Workers' Rights

Workers have the right to:

- Working conditions that do not pose a risk of serious harm.
- Receive information and training (in a language and vocabulary the worker understands) about workplace hazards, methods to prevent them, and the OSHA standards that apply to their workplace.
- Review records of work-related injuries and illnesses.
- File a complaint asking OSHA to inspect their workplace if they believe there is a serious hazard or that their employer is not following OSHA's rules. OSHA will keep all identities confidential.
- Exercise their rights under the law without retaliation, including reporting an injury or raising health and safety concerns with their employer or OSHA. If a worker has been retaliated against for using their rights, they must file a complaint with OSHA as soon as possible, but no later than 30 days.

For more information, see OSHA's Workers page.

OSHA Assistance, Services and Programs

OSHA has a great deal of information to assist employers in complying with their responsibilities under OSHA law. Several OSHA programs and services can help employers identify and correct job hazards, as well as improve their injury and illness prevention program.

Establishing an Injury and Illness Prevention Program

The key to a safe and healthful work environment is a comprehensive injury and illness prevention program.

Injury and illness prevention programs are systems that can substantially reduce the number and severity of workplace injuries and illnesses, while reducing costs to employers. Thousands of employers across the United States already manage safety using injury and illness prevention programs, and OSHA believes that all employers can and should do the same. Thirty-four states have requirements or voluntary guidelines for workplace injury and illness prevention programs. Most successful injury and illness prevention programs are based on a common set of key elements. These include management leadership, worker participation, hazard identification, hazard prevention and control, education and training, and program evaluation and improvement. Visit OSHA's Injury and Illness Prevention Programs web page at www.osha.gov/dsg/topics/safetyhealth for more information.

Compliance Assistance Specialists

OSHA has compliance assistance specialists throughout the nation located in most OSHA offices. Compliance assistance specialists can provide information to employers and workers about OSHA standards, short educational programs on specific hazards or OSHA rights and responsibilities, and information on additional compliance assistance resources. For more details, visit www.osha.gov/dcsp/compliance_assistance/cas.html or call 1-800-321-OSHA (6742) to contact your local OSHA office.

Free On-site Safety and Health Consultation Services for Small Business

OSHA's On-site Consultation Program offers free and confidential advice to small and medium-sized businesses in all states across the country, with priority given to high-hazard worksites. Each year, responding to requests from small employers looking to create or improve their safety and health management programs, OSHA's On-site Consultation Program conducts over 29,000 visits to small business worksites covering over 1.5 million workers across the nation.

On-site consultation services are separate from enforcement and do not result in penalties or citations. Consultants from state agencies or universities work with employers to identify workplace hazards, provide advice on compliance with OSHA standards, and assist in establishing safety and health management programs.

For more information, to find the local On-site Consultation office in your state, or to request a brochure on Consultation Services, visit www.osha.gov/consultation, or call 1-800-321-OSHA (6742).

Under the consultation program, certain exemplary employers may request participation in OSHA's **Safety and Health Achievement Recognition Program (SHARP)**. Eligibility for participation includes, but is not limited to, receiving a full-service, comprehensive consultation visit, correcting all identified hazards and developing an effective safety and health management program. Worksites that receive SHARP recognition are exempt from programmed inspections during the period that the SHARP certification is valid.

Occupational Safety and Health Training Courses

The OSHA Training Institute partners with 27 OSHA Training Institute Education Centers at 42 locations throughout the United States to deliver courses on OSHA standards and occupational safety and health topics to thousands of students a year. For more information on training courses, visit www.osha.gov/otiec.

OSHA Educational Materials

OSHA has many types of educational materials in English, Spanish, Vietnamese and other languages available in print or online. These include:

- Brochures/booklets;
- Fact Sheets;
- Guidance documents that provide detailed examinations of specific safety and health issues;
- Online Safety and Health Topics pages;
- Posters;
- Small, laminated QuickCards™ that provide brief safety and health information; and
- *QuickTakes*, OSHA's free, twice-monthly online newsletter with the latest news about OSHA initiatives and products to assist employers and workers in finding and preventing

workplace hazards. To sign up for *QuickTakes* visit www.osha. gov/quicktakes.

To view materials available online or for a listing of free publications, visit www.osha.gov/publications. You can also call 1-800-321-OSHA (6742) to order publications.

OSHA's web site also has information on job hazards and injury and illness prevention for employers and workers. To learn more about OSHA's safety and health resources online, visit www.osha.gov. Use the A-Z index to help find information and assistance.

NIOSH Health Hazard Evaluation Program

Getting Help with Health Hazards

The National Institute for Occupational Safety and Health (NIOSH) is a federal agency that conducts scientific and medical research on workers' safety and health. At no cost to employers or workers, NIOSH can help identify health hazards and recommend ways to reduce or eliminate those hazards in the workplace through its Health Hazard Evaluation (HHE) Program.

Workers, union representatives and employers can request a NIOSH HHE. An HHE is often requested when there is a higher than expected rate of a disease or injury in a group of workers. These situations may be the result of an unknown cause, a new hazard, or a mixture of sources. To request a NIOSH Health Hazard Evaluation go to www.cdc.gov/niosh/hhe/request.html. To find out more about the Health Hazard Evaluation Program:

- Call (513) 841-4382, or to talk to a staff member in Spanish, call (513) 841-4439; or
- Send an email to HHERequestHelp@cdc.gov.

OSHA Regional Offices

Region I
Boston Regional Office

(CT*, ME, MA, NH, RI, VT*)
JFK Federal Building, Room E340
Boston, MA 02203
(617) 565-9860 (617) 565-9827 Fax

Region II
New York Regional Office
(NJ*, NY*, PR*, VI*)
201 Varick Street, Room 670
New York, NY 10014
(212) 337-2378 (212) 337-2371 Fax

Region III
Philadelphia Regional Office
(DE, DC, MD*, PA, VA*, WV)
The Curtis Center
170 S. Independence Mall West
Suite 740 West
Philadelphia, PA 19106-3309
(215) 861-4900 (215) 861-4904 Fax

Region IV
Atlanta Regional Office
(AL, FL, GA, KY*, MS, NC*, SC*, TN*)
61 Forsyth Street, SW, Room 6T50
Atlanta, GA 30303
(678) 237-0400 (678) 237-0447 Fax

Region V
Chicago Regional Office
(IL*, IN*, MI*, MN*, OH, WI)
230 South Dearborn Street
Room 3244
Chicago, IL 60604
(312) 353-2220 (312) 353-7774 Fax

Region VI
Dallas Regional Office
(AR, LA, NM*, OK, TX)

525 Griffin Street, Room 602
Dallas, TX 75202
(972) 850-4145 (972) 850-4149 Fax
(972) 850-4150 FSO Fax

Region VII
Kansas City Regional Office
(IA*, KS, MO, NE)
Two Pershing Square Building
2300 Main Street, Suite 1010
Kansas City, MO 64108-2416
(816) 283-8745 (816) 283-0547 Fax

Region VIII
Denver Regional Office
(CO, MT, ND, SD, UT*, WY*)
Cesar Chavez Memorial Building
1244 Speer Boulevard, Suite 551
Denver, CO 80204
(720) 264-6550 (720) 264-6585 Fax

Region IX
San Francisco Regional Office
(AZ*, CA*, HI*, NV*, and American Samoa,
Guam and the Northern Mariana Islands)
90 7th Street, Suite 18100
San Francisco, CA 94103
(415) 625-2547 (415) 625-2534 Fax

Region X
Seattle Regional Office
(AK*, ID, OR*, WA*)
300 Fifth Avenue, Suite 1280
Seattle, WA 98104
(206) 757-6700 (206) 757-6705 Fax

* These states and territories operate their own OSHA-
approved job safety and health plans and cover state and local
government employees as well as private sector employees.
The Connecticut, Illinois, New Jersey, New York and Virgin

Islands programs cover public employees only. (Private sector workers in these states are covered by Federal OSHA). States with approved programs must have standards that are identical to, or at least as effective as, the Federal OSHA standards.

Note: To get contact information for OSHA area offices, OSHA-approved state plans and OSHA consultation projects, please visit us online at www.osha.gov or call us at 1-800-321-OSHA (6742).

How to Contact OSHA

For questions or to get information or advice, to report an emergency, report a fatality or catastrophe, order publications, sign up for OSHA's e-newsletter *QuickTakes*, or to file a confidential complaint, contact your nearest OSHA office, visit www.osha.gov or call OSHA at 1-800-321-OSHA (6742), TTY 1-877-889-5627.

For assistance, contact us.
We are OSHA. We can help.